PLASMA NEON DREAM

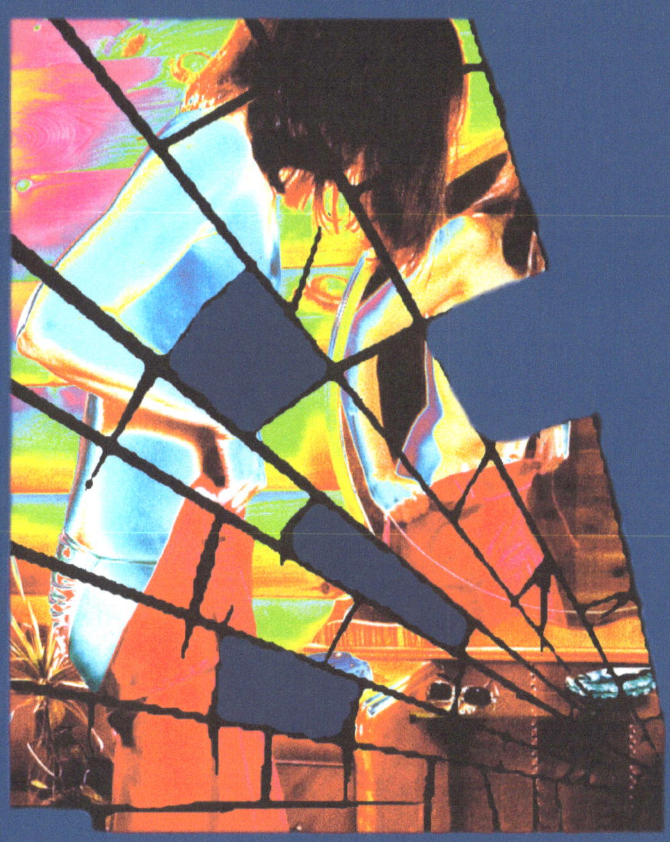

Jy Chiperzak

Dreaming...

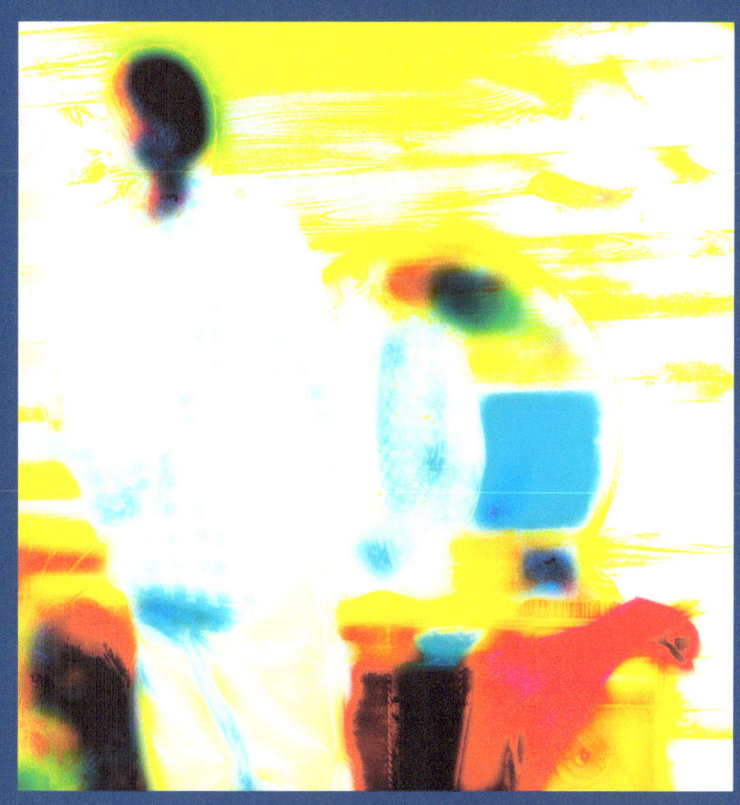

A yang pose questioning what she isn't.

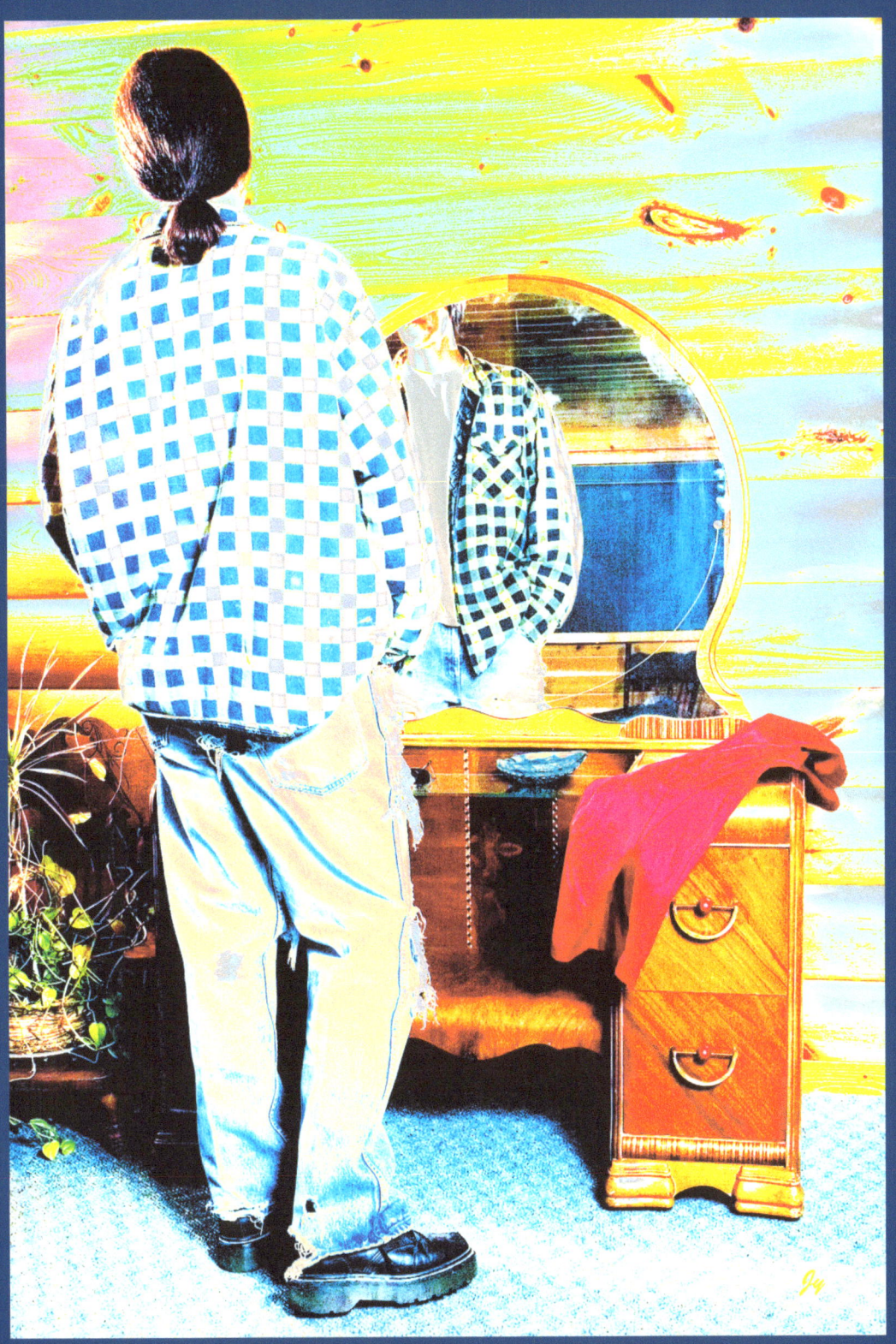

A man? A woman? A girl in boys clothes?

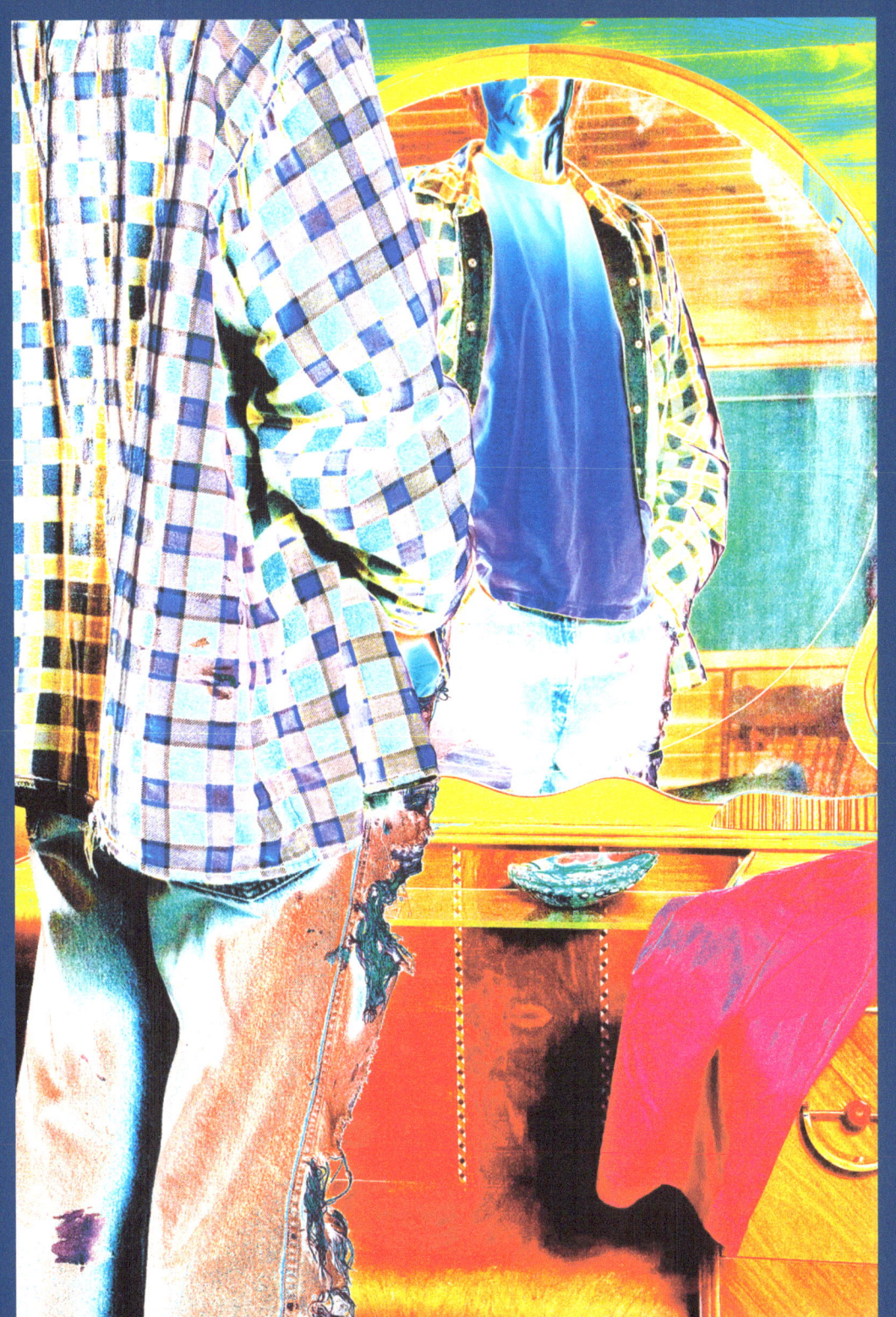

What is outer? What is inner?
The body? The mind?

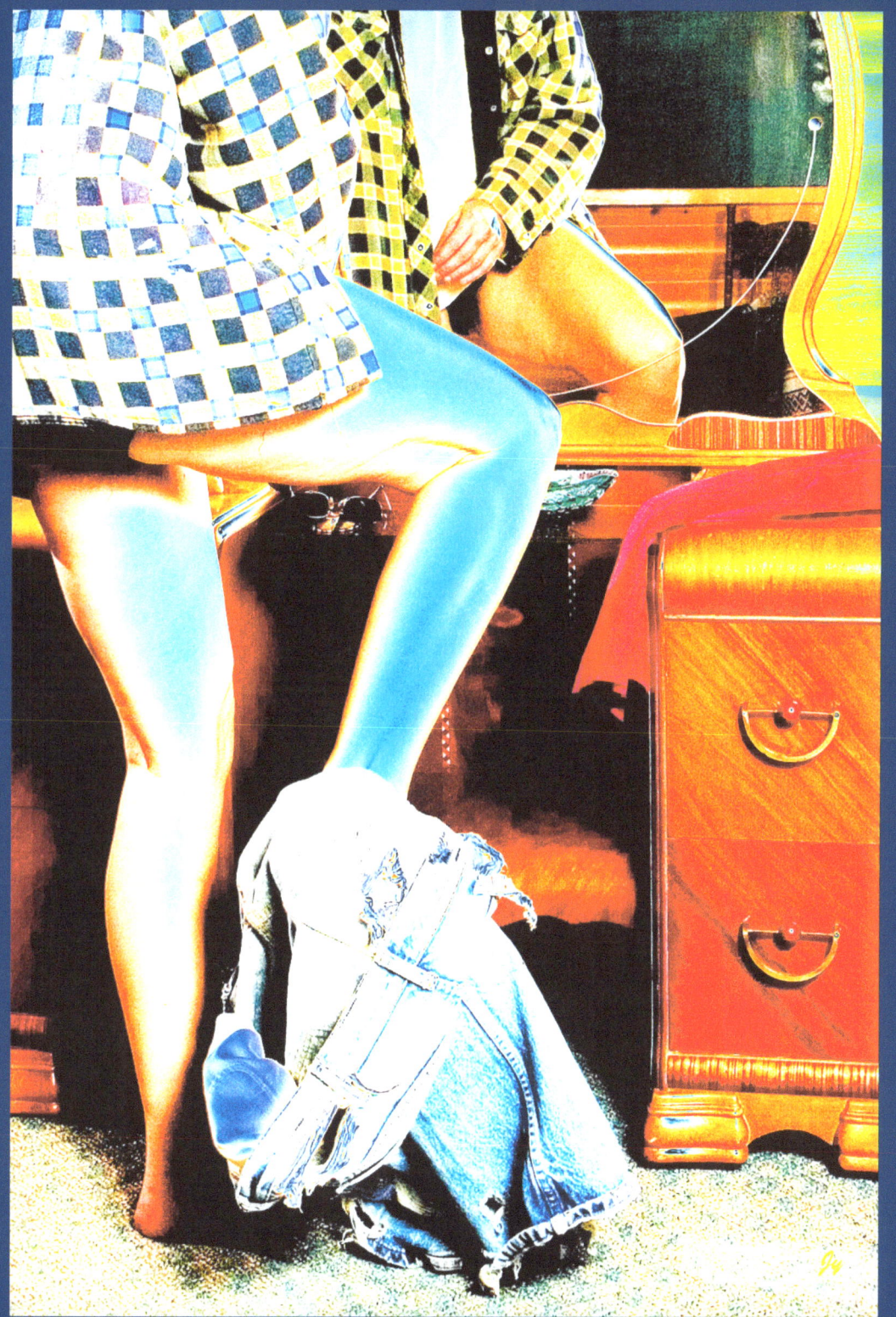

What others see… perceptions
What she sees, the intimate mirror staring back.

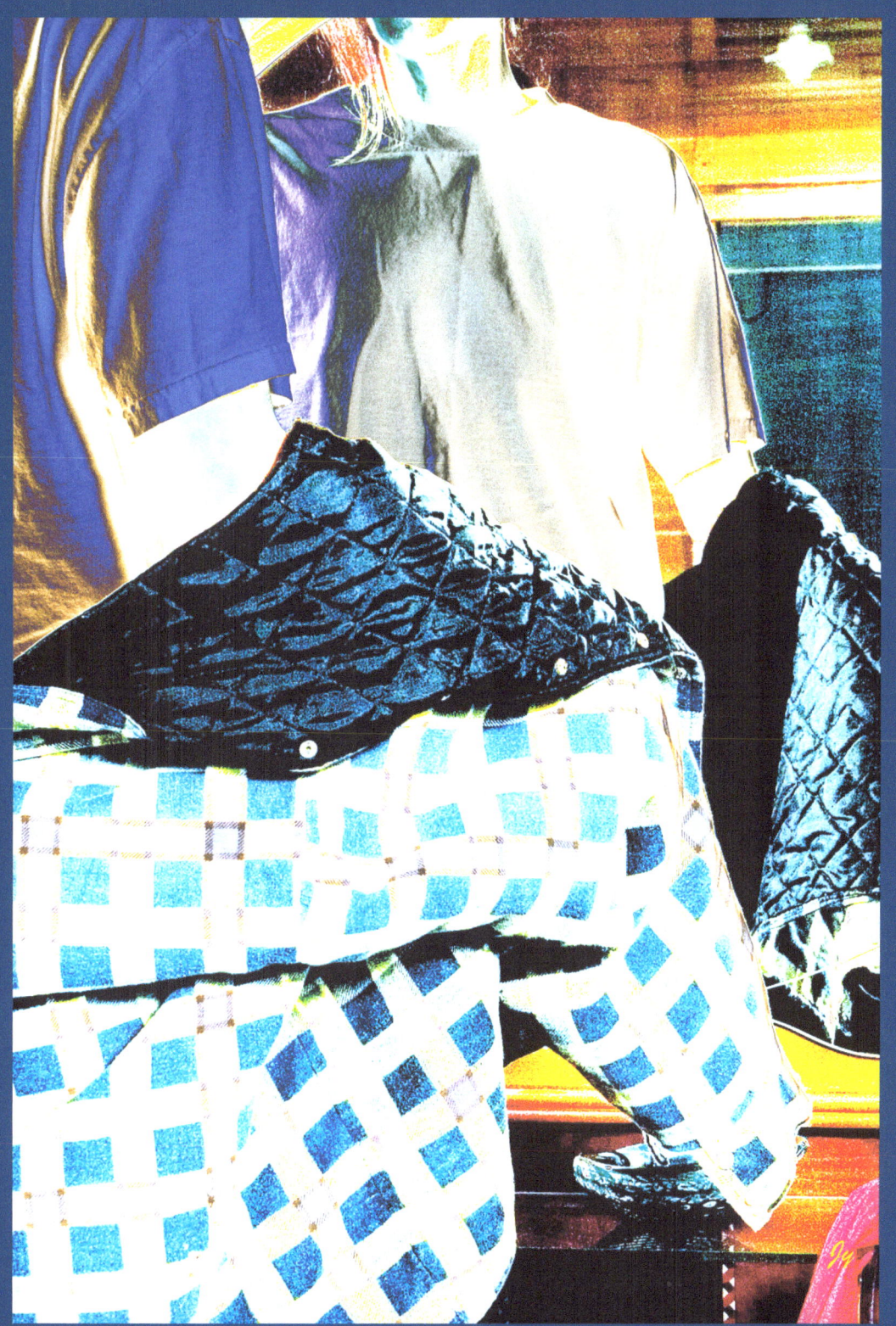

How do these illusions cohere
From neon dreaming
To the street world of life?

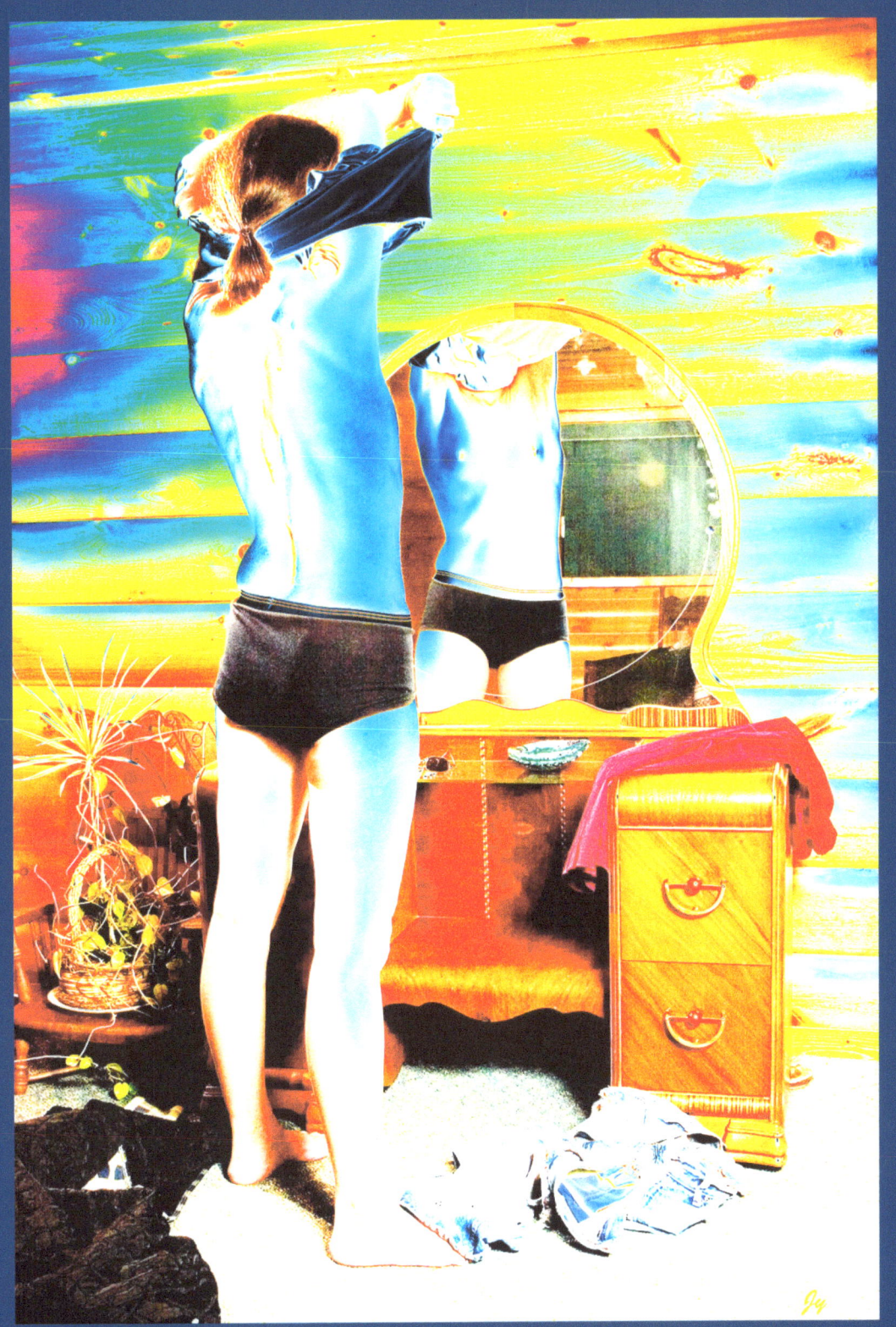

From she who stands outside
To she in the mirror looking out.

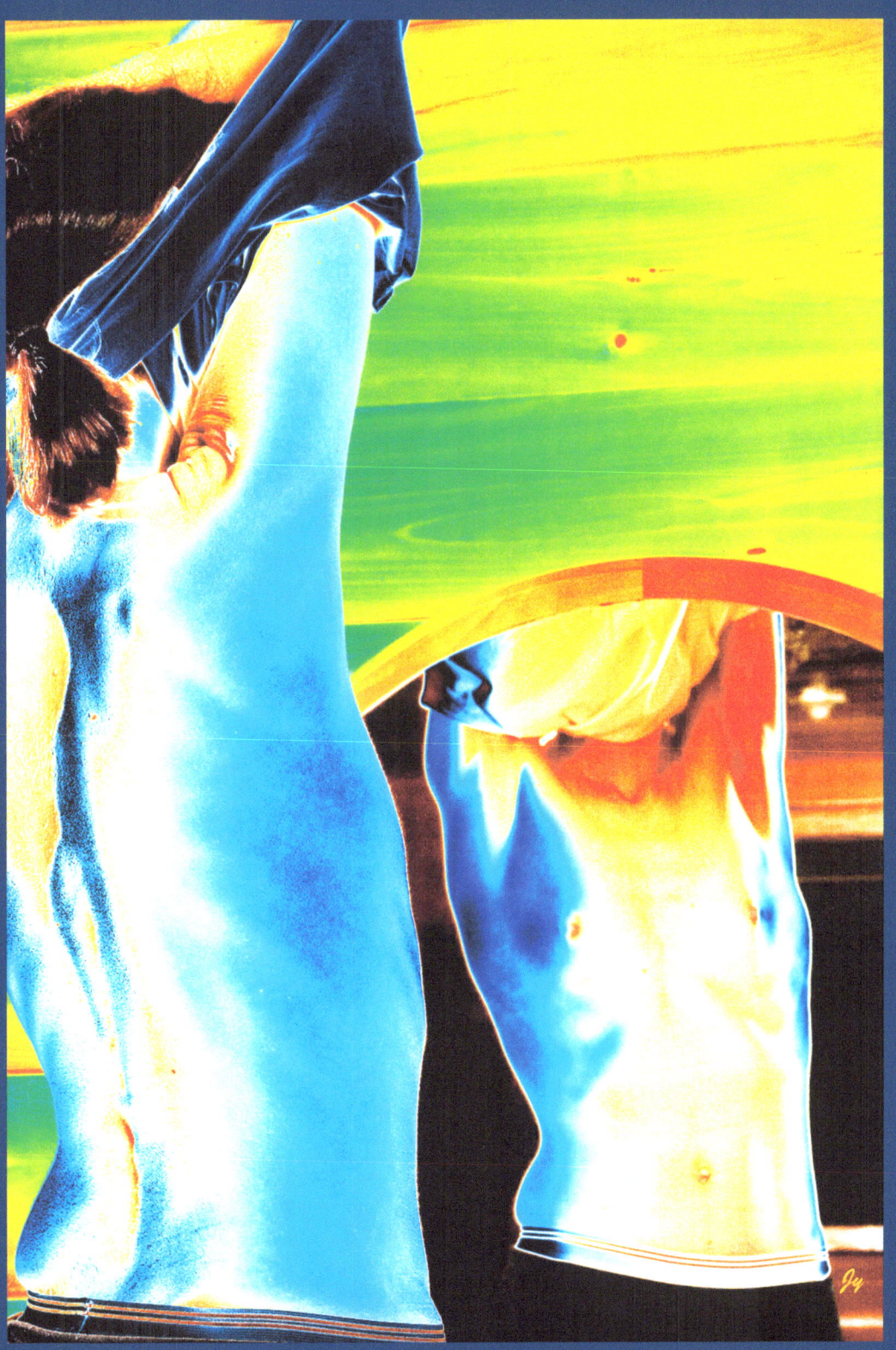

Will they, can they
Become one with each other
A boundary crossed?
She watches…

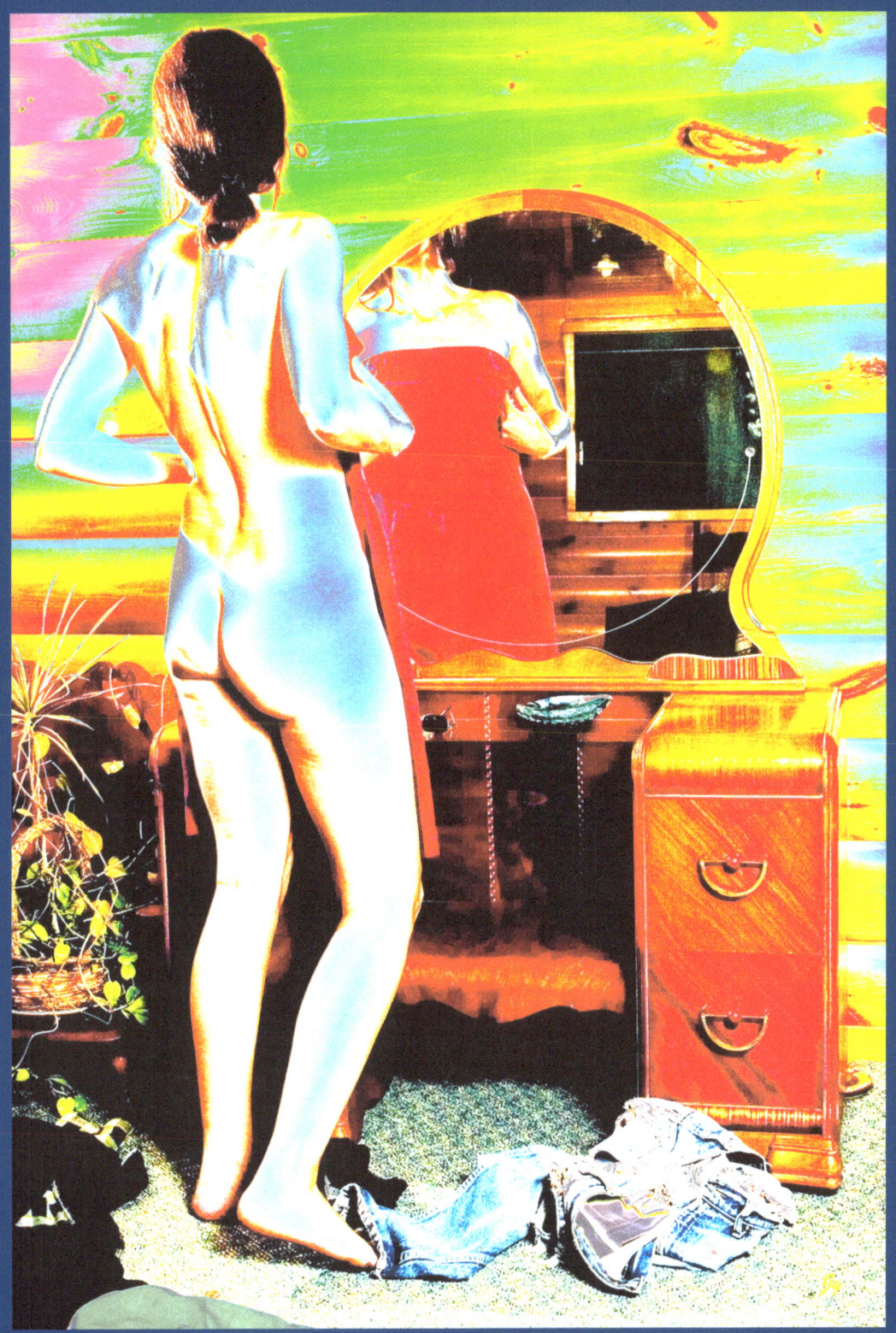

The colour is red… passion
Beyond questions, beyond intellect
Burning.

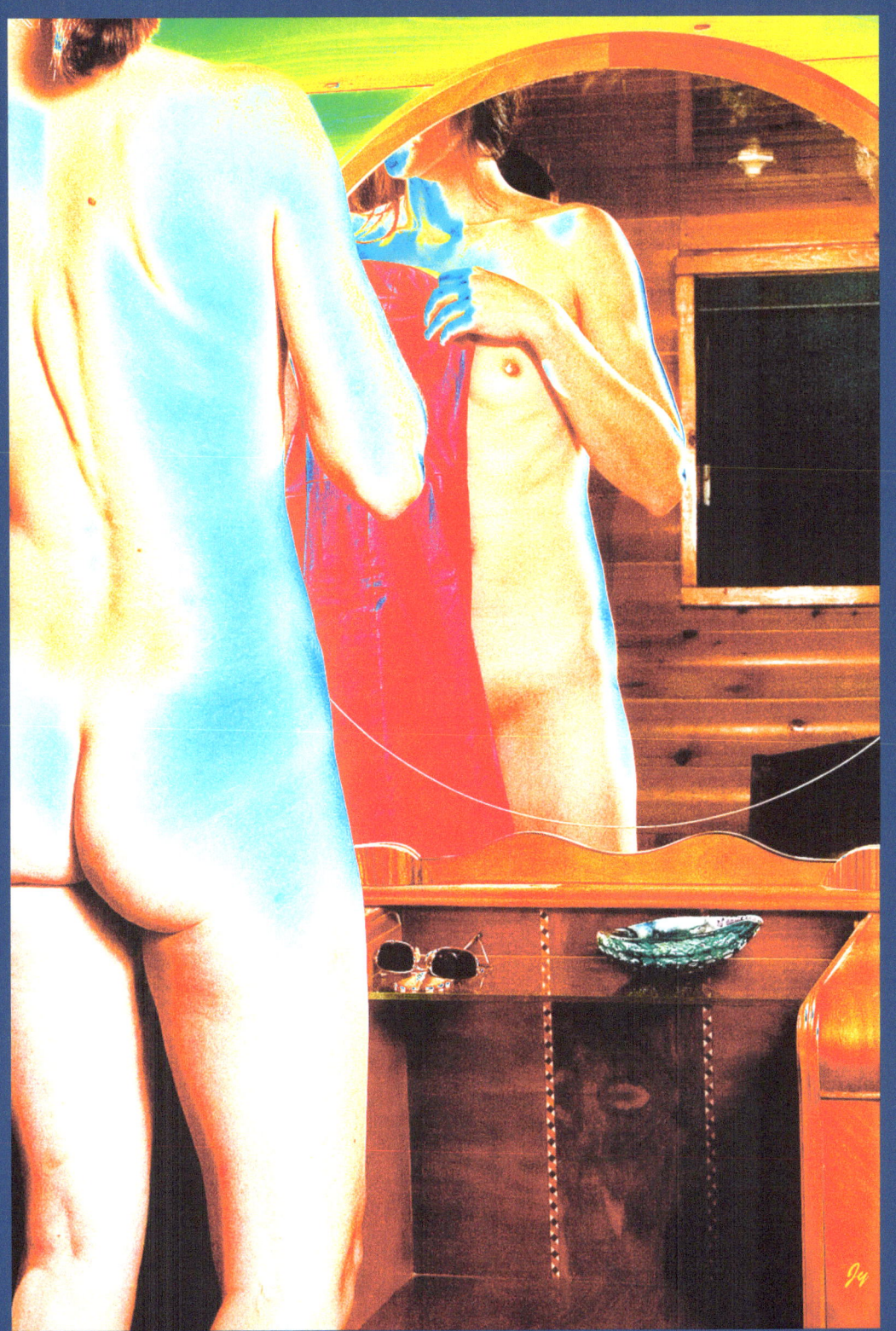

She watches the mirror
Her body glows strange
Plasma Neon.

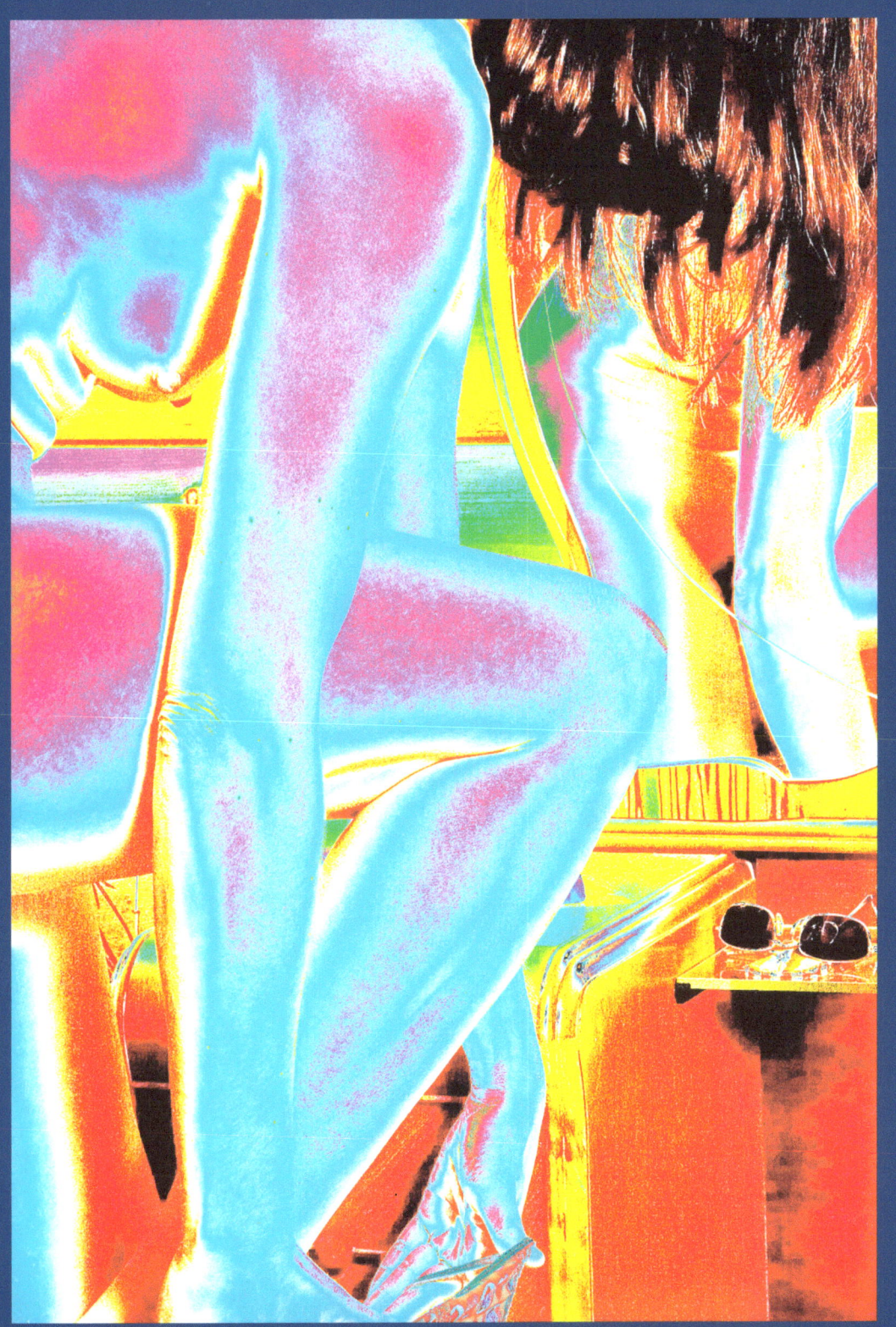

In this heat of transformation
She wonders a cover up, a lie.

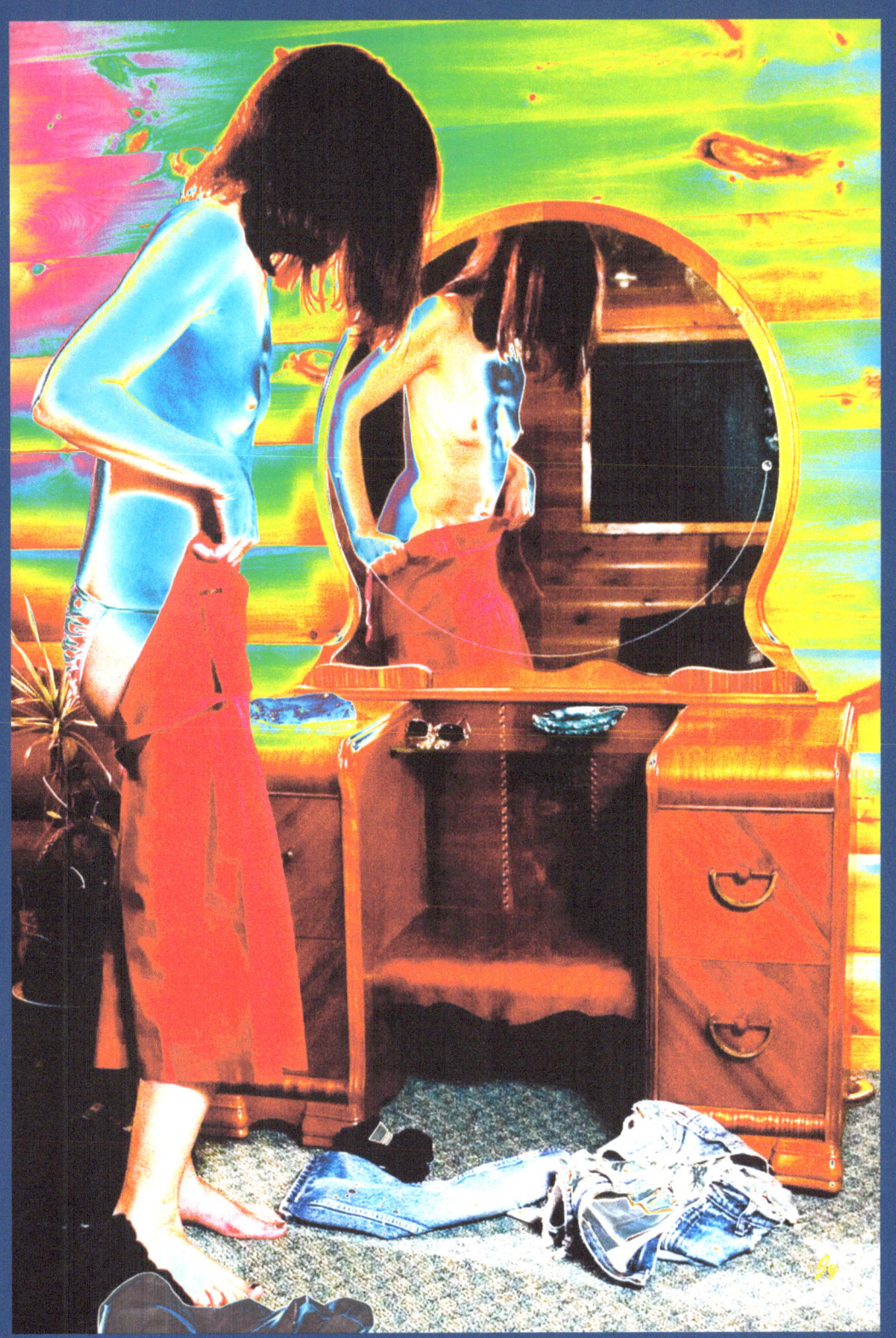

Just another illusion
Hiding what is within.

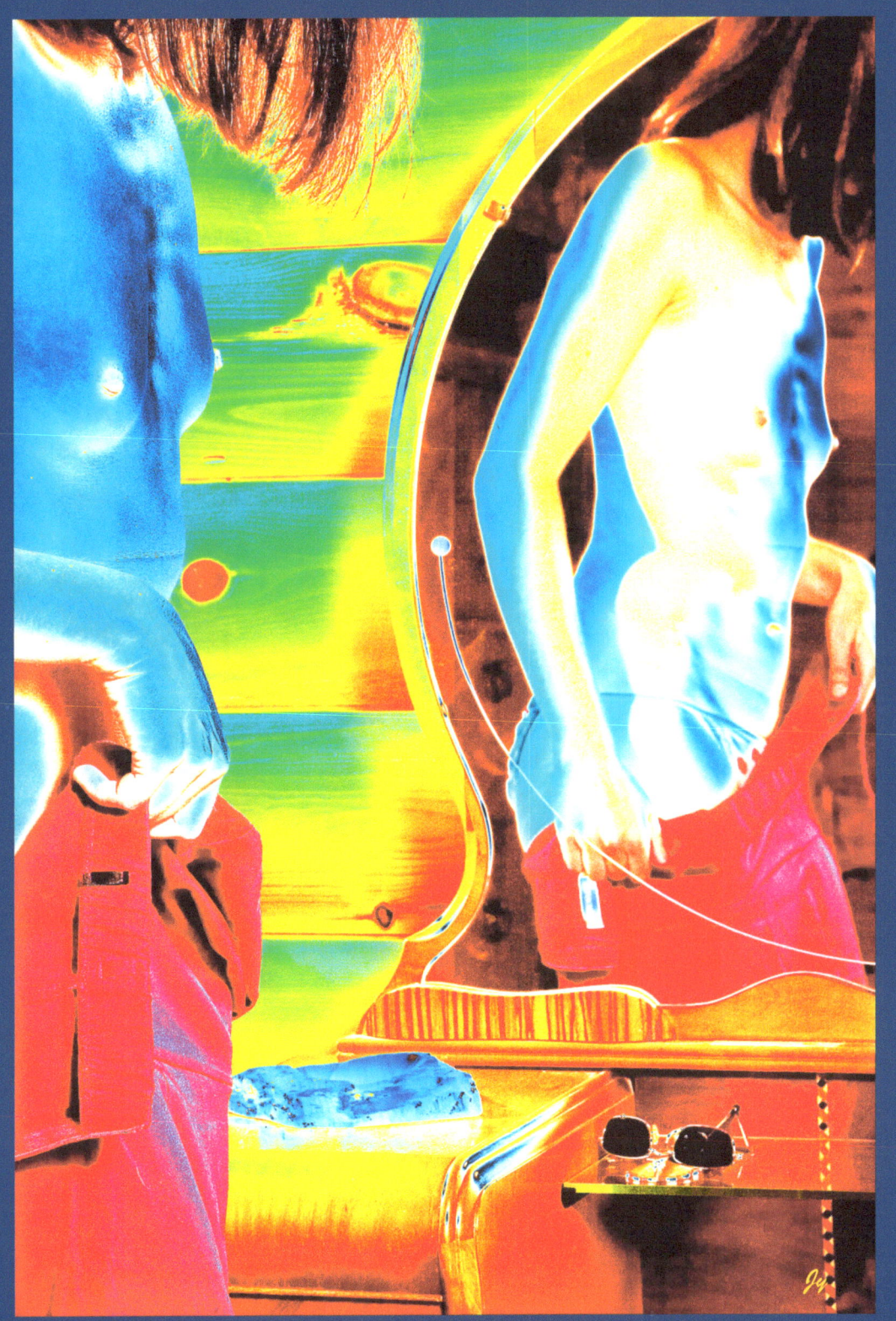

But woman to woman
The mirror whispers…

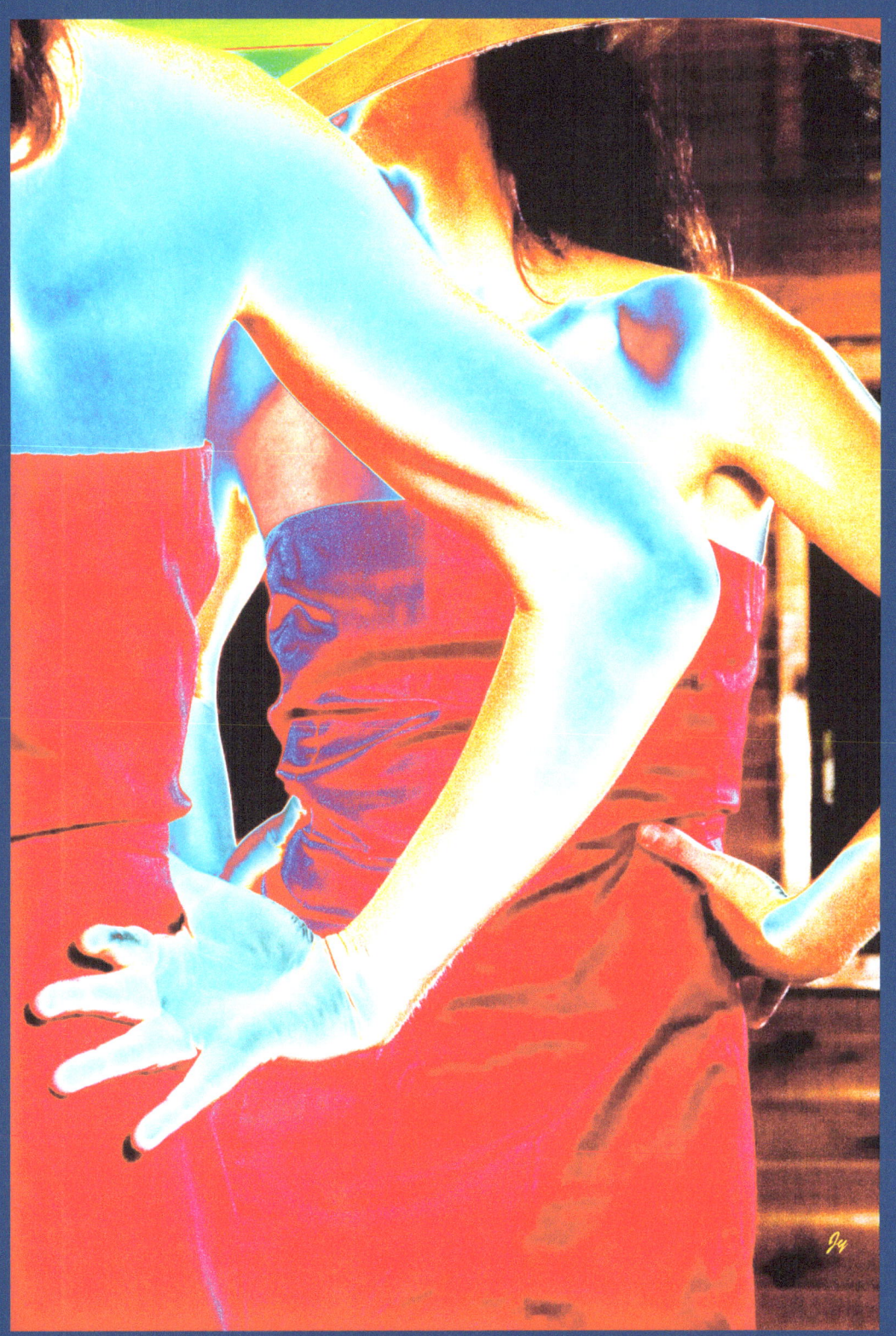

Go, strike out, strike out
From this bright dream.

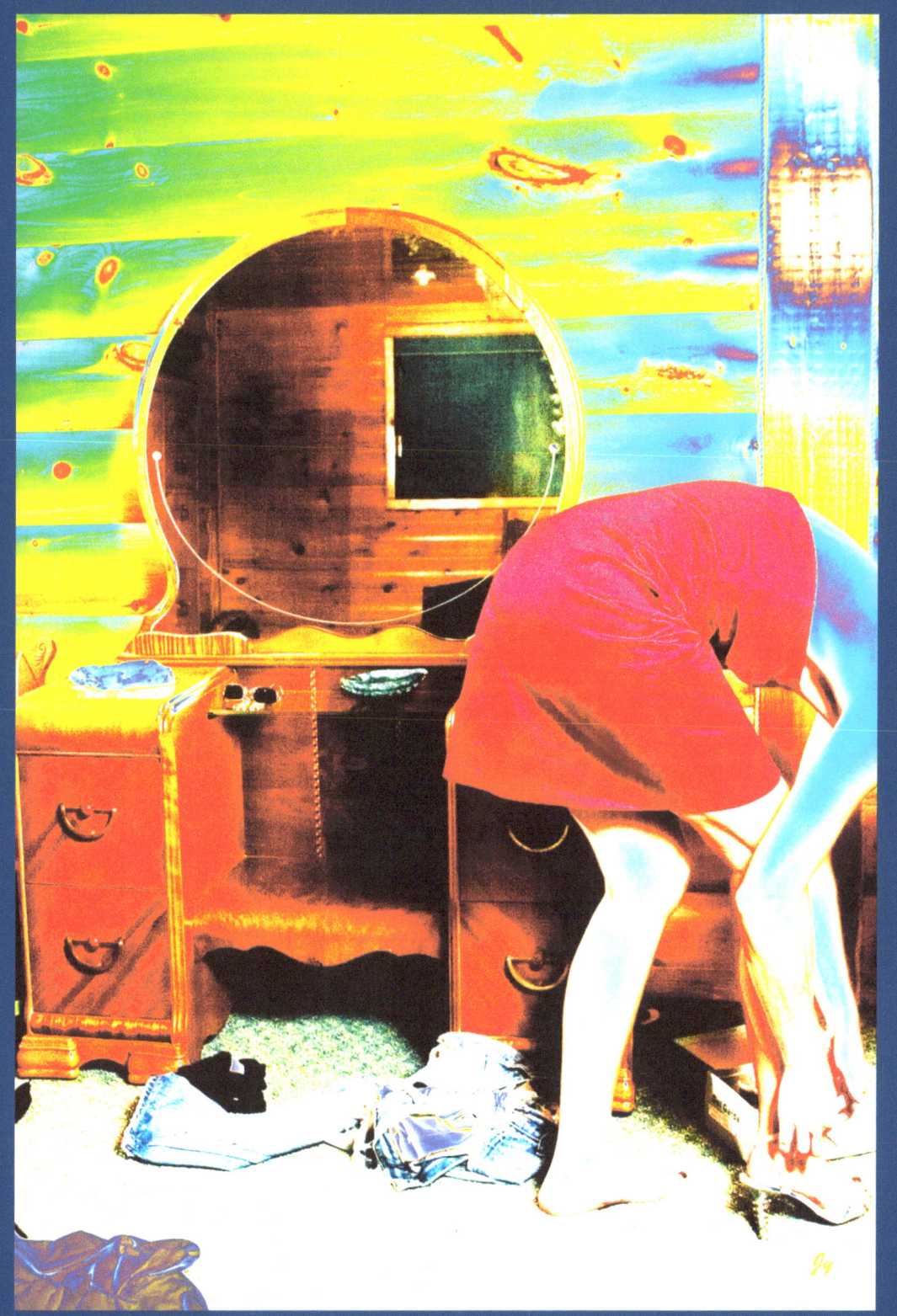

Walking on to new perceptions
Hers, theirs yet to discover
She awakens.

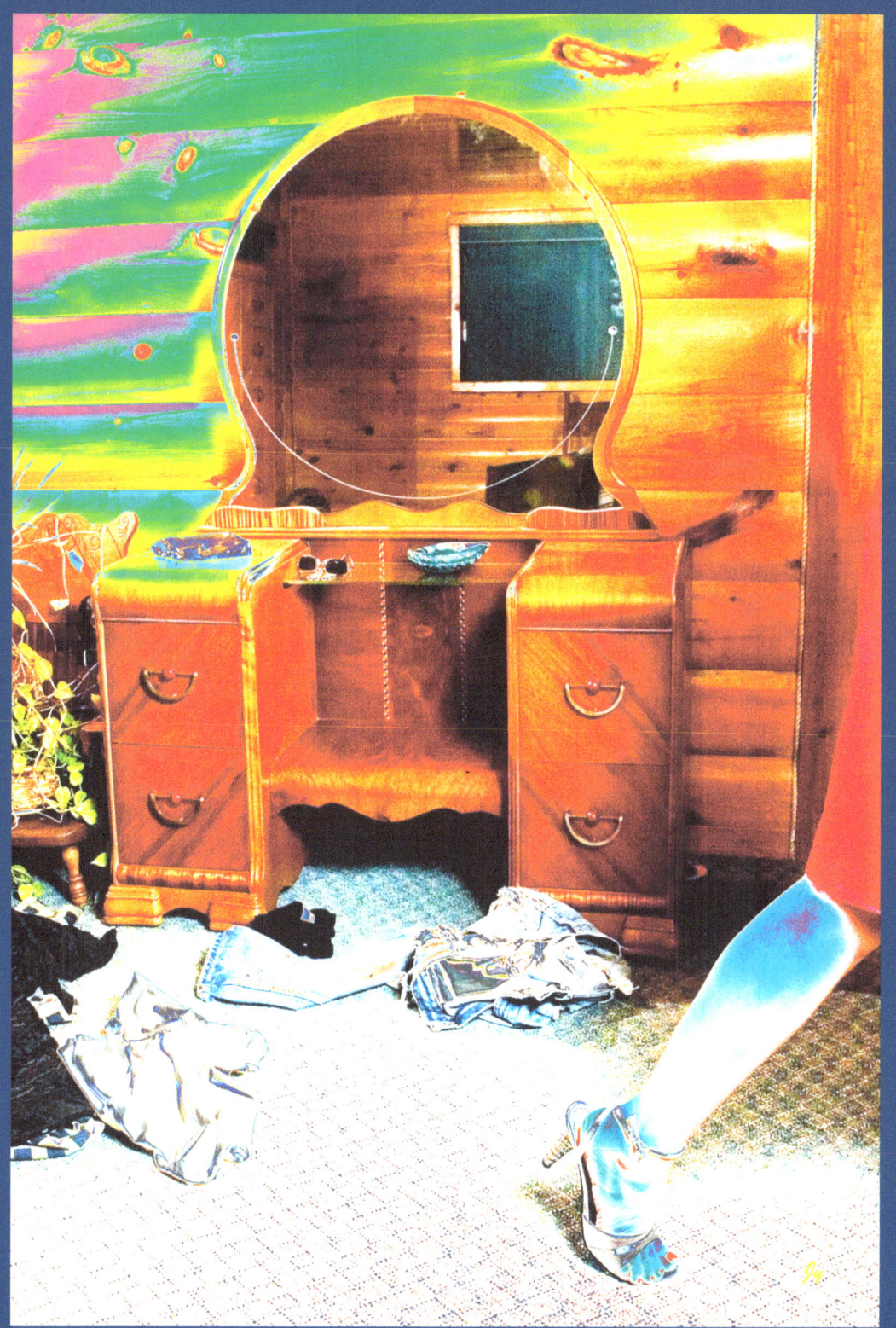

the end...

and now...

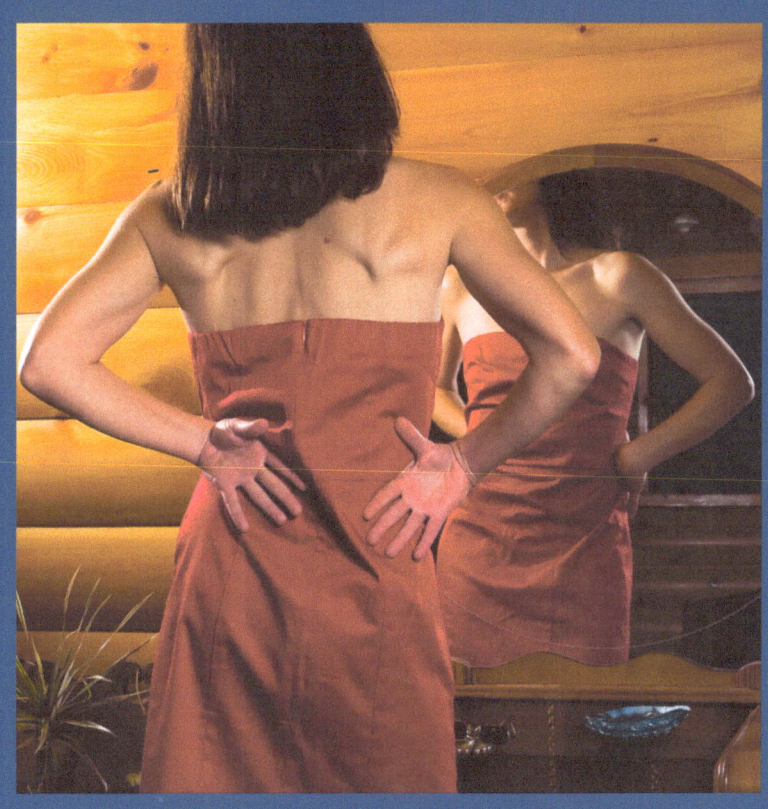

Jy Chiperzak

Since age 12 the camera has been the one constant tool in my life. Professionally, I studied film at the London School of Film Technology, England. My pursuits were multi faceted, from the Montreal underground film and art scene to freelance directing and producing for CBC's *the Nature of Things* in conjunction with the National Film Board of Canada.

I've since returned to the still image but with new eyes… a wanting to see beyond the everyday borders of space, color, object. I endeavour to look beyond a reality that is constrained not only physically by the limitations of the receptors in our eyes, but by our own psyches and emotions… our subjectivity.

Digital imagery is my way of returning to my artistic roots, photography. It provides the tools to reinterpret the realities of my experiential/emotional realms, an altered seeing of the inner/outer world around me.

Plasma Neon Dream
Copyright © Jy Chipersak, 2012

ISBN (book): 978-0-9878019-0-6
ISBN (e-book): 978-0-9878019-1-3

CIP available

Published by
Why Knot Books
5443 Eighth Line,
Erin, ON, N0B 1T0
Canada
Editorial: 519-833-1242
Distribution: Jason Dickson, 705-646-2215

www.ingramcontent.com/pod-product-compliance
Lightning Source LLC
Chambersburg PA
CBHW050406180526
45159CB00005B/2171